COUNTRY
PAINTING
·PROJECTS·

COUNTRY
PAINTING
·PROJECTS·

decorating on wood, pottery, and metal

EMMA HUNK

THE READER'S DIGEST ASSOCIATION, INC.
Pleasantville, New York/Montreal

A READER'S DIGEST BOOK

Edited and produced by David & Charles Publishers
Photography by Shona Wood, *Book design by* Diana Knapp

First published in Great Britain in 1996

Library of Congress Cataloging in Publication Data

Hunk, Emma.
    Country painting projects: decorating on wood, pottery, and metal
/ Emma Hunk,
        p.   cm.
    Includes index.
    ISBN 0-89577-910-2
    1. Painting. 2. Decoration and ornament, Rustic.   I. Title.
TT385.H86   1997
745.7′23—dc20   96-2265 1
                                                              CIP

Printed in the United States
Second Printing, April 1997

CONTENTS

INTRODUCTION

During the mid-1980s, I lived in North America and I was continually intrigued by the painted crafts and accessories on display and available just about everywhere. Muted and apparently antique colors were combined with charming naive motifs stenciled onto everything from Shaker-style boxes to chests of drawers. I had always had an interest in arts and crafts but had no formal training and lacked sufficient confidence in my abilities. I would admire many of the items and, like so many others, think, "I could do that." But, again like so many others, I never found the time to try, persuading myself that there must be some secret ingredient that I didn't know about. Anyway, how much safer to think that you could do it but never find the time to try (and risk possible failure).

Almost a decade later, I have become a painting addict. As soon as I first saw a demonstration of a simple stenciling technique and realized that I really could do it, I was hooked. A friend then gave me a crash course in decorative painting techniques, and from that moment on, nothing in our house was safe from the paintbrush. I soon learned just how wonderful stenciling is in that it enabled me to produce consistently professional designs (initially, thanks to the clever stencil designers and manufacturers). Practice with the stencils and stencil paints soon led me into simple shading and highlighting techniques, which transforms a flat design into something that is three-dimensional and alive.

I very much hope that this book will help to release the artist trapped inside you. I don't know how many times I've overheard people looking at my work saying, "It's very nice, but I could never do that." I'm sure that they could, and this book aims to show you how to paint a simple household item and turn it into something that you can be proud of.

I have tried to make the designs and techniques as simple and straightforward as possible, and the items to paint are inexpensive. There are some pieces of equipment and artist's materials that I do highly recommend for the projects, and some of these can seem costly, especially when purchased together. If taken care of, however, the equipment that you buy will last a long time and give you a great deal of pleasure and satisfaction.

Happy painting!

OPPOSITE   To make any of the objects in this book, you require only the minimal amount of materials.

MATERIALS &

MATERIALS AND PAINTS

When you are painting your chosen object, a few other materials are useful in addition to the items listed below. Always have clean, soft rags on hand to clean up spills of paint or water, or background runs and drips. Some small white saucers or plates for mixing paints also come in handy.

BRUSHES

To create any of the designs in this book, you will need only a few paintbrushes. For backgrounds, use a good-quality 1½in- (3.5cm-) wide flat paintbrush. The better the quality, the less likely you are to have stray bristles falling out of the brush and getting stuck in your meticulously executed paintwork.

To apply the motifs through a stencil, use a stencil brush. You will need one that is approximately ½in (12mm) wide, as this is the size most adaptable to any size stencil. For smaller stencil details, a ¼in (6mm) brush may be needed. Then, for the detail work, I recommend just three sizes of artist's paintbrushes—Nos. 1, 4, and 6. Armed with these three brushes, you will be able to paint detailed and larger areas of color equally well.

Always clean your paintbrushes thoroughly. This will keep them in good condition and ensure that the next color you use is not tainted by the previous color. For brushes that have been used with oil-

TECHNIQUES

based paints, massage some mineral spirits or paint thinner followed by Murphy's Oil Soap into the bristles to get rid of the oily residue. Those that have been used with water-based paints need only to be washed in some detergent, such as dish-washing liquid, and then rinsed thoroughly in tap water.

PAINTS

On wooden and terracotta surfaces I use acrylics or latex paints. These water-based paints are great to work with as they dry quite quickly. When painting the motifs, I tend to use acrylic paints. You can mix acrylic and latex paints together should you need to. Use water to thin these paints.

For backgrounds on metal or enamel projects, I use satin-finish oil-based paint. Never use gloss as the resultant surface is too shiny. For the motifs, use artists' oils. To thin oil-based paints, use either mineral spirits or turpentine depending on the manufacturer's recommendation. Oil-based paints are a little trickier to use than water-based because they take a long time to dry. Make sure each stage is thoroughly dry before putting on another layer. Adding a product called Liquin to your paints speeds the drying time, but it gives a slightly less opaque finish.

If you have not painted before, it is a good idea to start with a project which uses water-based paints, as many people find them easier to use. I often use acrylic paints instead of artists' oils to

Painting materials (counterclockwise from top left): artist's paintbrushes, stencil paintbrushes, oil and acrylic paints, flat paintbrush, chalk, pencils, and varnish.

stencil and paint the motifs on to a satin-finish oil-based background to avoid the lengthy drying time required for artists' oil. Although mixing latex and oil paints is not recommended by the manufacturers, I have yet to have a failure using them in this way.

Several of the projects in this book feature gold paint. After much experimenting, I have found that an oil-based gold is the best type of paint to use. However, varnishing over gold oil paint can be difficult, and it is very important that you let the paint dry for at least an hour longer than you would normally. When you then apply the varnish, don't paint over it with too many brush strokes, as the gold can wear off very easily and look tarnished.

ANTIQUING MEDIUM

Antiquing an object can be a very good way to finish it. It gives a suitably aged look, very much in harmony with my designs. Antiquing medium is widely available; you paint it on as directed by the manufacturer and varnish it when dry.

Alternatively, make your own antiquing medium. Into an egg cup filled with varnish, add a drop of raw umber oil paint (about the size of a pinhead) and mix together. Before applying the liquid, test it on a similarly painted surface to check that the color is right. Then apply the liquid to the surface using either a soft cloth or a paintbrush and wipe off with a soft cloth. It is preferable to use a paintbrush, as it is easier to get the liquid into small corners.

VARNISHES

A coat of varnish will give your painted object a tough finish, ensuring that it lasts a long time and will protect water-based paints from smudging if the object comes into contact with water. Based on which material the object is made of, various types of varnishes are available. For wooden items on which acrylic or latex paint has been used as a base coat, use an acrylic varnish. It is quick drying and is available in gloss or matte depending on the finish you are looking for. Otherwise, use a polyurethane varnish, which gives a harder finish.

CHALK AND PENCIL

Chalk is particularly useful if you need to draw on a larger, awkward surface, such as around the curve of a galvanized bucket. It is also preferable to use chalk rather than pencil on an oil-based paint surface, as it will show up better. However, for finer details, where you need a sharper image, use pencil.

STENCILING MATERIALS

Preparing and using a stencil is explained in greater detail on pages 14–15, but below is a list of the essential materials:

Stenciling materials (from top left): repositionable spray glue, cut acetate, craft knife and protective cover, masking tape, marker pen, and roll of sheet acetate. All of these materials are resting on a cutting mat.

SHEET ACETATE OR STENCIL BOARD

Either of these materials can be used to cut the stencils from. However, I prefer to use acetate (and that is what I recommend throughout this book). Acetate is transparent. This makes it easier to check that the motif is correctly positioned. This material is more malleable, making it good for covering lumps and bumps that might exist in the surface background.

MARKER PEN

It is best to use a fine-nibbed marker pen so that you can transfer the motif very accurately.

CUTTING MAT

Professional cutting mats are available from art supply stores. They can be expensive, so they are worth buying only if you are planning on doing a lot of stenciling. Alternatively, use plate glass with masking tape wrapped around the edges, or a thick sheet of cardboard, to prevent any accidents. If you are going to use the latter, make sure that it is very smooth, with no previous cutting lines in it, as this could affect the way in which the craft knife cuts the new stencil.

MASKING TAPE

Masking tape is invaluable for stenciling because it can be reused so easily. In addition to holding a stencil in place when you cut out, the tape can also be used to hold the stencil in place when you paint over it. Masking tape is ideal for covering up parts of a design that you don't necessarily want to stencil through.

CRAFT KNIFE

These sharp knives are the only blades to use when cutting out a stencil. A small pair of sharp embroidery scissors can be used for more intricate work; but to cut with smooth, long, flowing lines, use the craft knife.

REPOSITIONABLE SPRAY GLUE

This sort of glue is wonderful for keeping a stencil in place when painting through it. Some people prefer to hold the stencil in place or to use masking tape instead, but for the best results, use repositionable spray glue. With the glue, the whole stencil will adhere well, eliminating the possibility of paint running down behind the acetate. It also leaves the hands free for painting.

PREPARATION OF OBJECTS

WOOD

Particularly if the object is old, you will need to sand down any rough parts or edges before beginning to paint. The occasional lump in the woodwork doesn't really matter for designs like mine, as they add to the charm of the finished piece. So don't feel that you must achieve the smoothest possible surface. After you have finished sanding, wipe the object with a damp cloth and then let it dry thoroughly before you begin to paint.

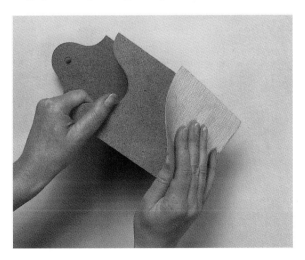

TERRACOTTA

Apart from making sure that any terracotta plant pots that you use are clean and dry (this is particu-

larly the case if the pots have been left in the garden for some time), there is really no preparation required for these items.

METAL

For objects like the galvanized metal watering can and bread box used in this book, you need to remove any bits of rust with sandpaper or steel wool before you begin to paint. Also, these objects frequently have labels stuck to them. Use mineral spirits or Murphy's Oil Soap on a soft, clean cloth to remove any residue left from peeling off the labels. Then, wipe the object with a damp cloth and let it dry thoroughly. It is a good idea to apply a coat of metal primer before beginning to paint.

PAINTING TECHNIQUES

APPLYING PAINT TO SURFACES

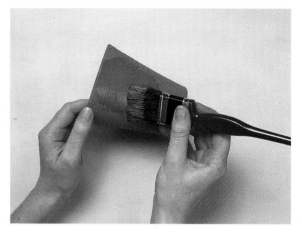

1 For the base coat of any object, never use more than a small amount of paint at a time. Dip your brush into the paint by no more than ½in (12mm). Never, on any account, push the brush in right up to the hilt.

2 The best way to remove any excess paint is by pressing the bristles against the side of the can, not the rim where paint may dry and lumps could fall into the paint later on. Then you should apply the paint in short, even brush strokes.

SHADING AND HIGHLIGHTING

The techniques shown here use water-based paints. Use oil-based paints in the same way, but thin the paint with mineral spirits or turpentine instead of water.

SHADING

1 Using black paint and a wet paintbrush or watered-down paint, draw a line of paint along the underside of the motif, such as along the bottom of the goose's belly.

2 Using your finger or thumb, quickly blend in the line of paint, softening the color into the body to give a gradually shaded effect.

HIGHLIGHTING

1 Apply white paint exactly the same way as for shading, but slightly in from the edge of the motif.

2 Using your finger or thumb, quickly blend in the line to the required degree, as for shading.

STENCILS AND TEMPLATES

PREPARING A STENCIL

The materials needed for stenciling are listed on pages 10–11. Here I show you exactly how to make and use a stencil, using the motifs given at the back of this book on pages 118–126.

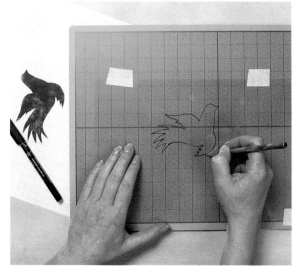

1 Photocopy your chosen design. If you do not have access to a photocopier, trace the motif from the book. Position a piece of acetate over the design and trace it off using a marker pen. Use pieces of masking tape to keep the acetate steady.

2 Fasten the acetate down onto your cutting mat and use the craft knife to cut out the motif. For safety, pull the craft knife away from your body, not toward it. Try to move the knife in long, flowing lines to ensure a neat edge.

3 If you should make a mistake when cutting out the stencil, the acetate can easily be repaired with Scotch tape. Spray the back of your stencil with repositionable glue, and position on your project.

4 Pick up a small amount of paint on your stencil brush, swirl around on a saucer to get bristles evenly coated. Then apply the paint to the stencil using a pouncing movement.

SIZING A STENCIL

If you don't want to use the outlines in exactly the same size as they are reproduced at the end of this book they are easy to alter.

The easiest way is to use a photocopier with enlarging and reducing facilities. You could also use a pantograph which copies a design, enlarging or reducing it in the process. There is also the good old-fashioned method of resizing by drawing squares over the existing outline. To enlarge the design, draw the same number of squares on a separate piece of paper, but much bigger. (The size depends on just how much you want to enlarge the design.) Then copy the design, transferring the lines exactly, square by square. To reduce the design, draw smaller squares.

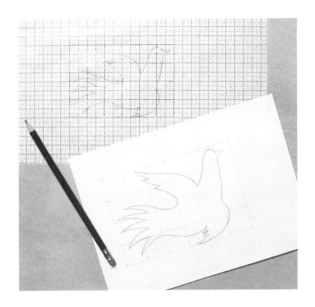

TEMPLATES

An alternative way of transferring the motif outline to your project is to make a cardboard template. There are two ways of doing this. One is to trace the motif from the back of the book onto thin cardboard using tracing paper, then cut around the outline using a craft knife or a pair of sharp scissors.

The other is to photocopy the motif from the back of the book and cut out the shape. Attach the paper shape to the card with small pieces of masking tape and draw around the outline. Cut out the motif shape from the card.

Size the motif up or down as for the stencil (see above). To use the template, spray the back of it with repositionable spray glue, position on your project and draw around the edge of the template using chalk.

BASIC BORDERS

Borders are the final embellishment on a project and can be tailored to your taste. Several different borders and motifs are shown below and opposite, together with simple instructions on how to paint them. Pencil or chalk in your border first, as this will make painting easier.

SIMPLE LEAF BORDER

A simple straight line with leaves radiating from it at regular intervals. Use mainly green paint, but dip into yellow occasionally to add natural-looking variation.

WAVY LEAF BORDER

The same principle as above, but make a gently undulating line first and then add the leaves.

FLOWER BORDER

Break up your leaf border with flowers. It is best to paint the flowers first and then join them together with leaves.

SUNFLOWER BORDER

Even though I have not used this border on the projects, it would be appropriate for a number of them. For this motif, use yellow paint to make a yellow disk with irregular edges and then add a raw umber center.

EGG-AND-LEAF BORDER

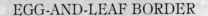

This egg-and-leaf border is appropriate with any of the fowl motifs. Because the egg shape
can be difficult to achieve freehand, it is advisable to make a stencil. Simply
stencil, paint, shade, and highlight your eggs as described in any of the projects
and then join together with the wavy leaf border.

LEMON BORDER

Follow the same directions as for the egg-and-leaf border above. Again, it would be useful to
make a lemon stencil. Pears are also attractive.

WHEAT BORDER

Follow the steps as shown above. Use a little brown paint with the yellow
to add some variation to the wheat color.

ABSTRACT BORDERS

Here are three simpler borders. Use them to decorate the edges and rims
of drawers and boxes.

SPOTTED PIG

The pig is an eternally popular farmyard animal. It also happens to be a very simple motif to paint, and the naive charm and rotund shape of this pig make it a perfect decoration for this inexpensive round tin tray (facing page). Pigs are also eminently suitable for buckets, sugar containers, bread boxes, and you can develop the simple outline into different colors and patterns. On the next two pages you will find more ideas for pig designs.

In the project that follows, I chose an old-fashioned "muddy" medium-blue for the background color. I avoided the predictable pink for the pig, choosing instead a creamy beige tone, which complements the antique blue. The finished item is both humorous and decorative, and the simple leaf-and-flower pattern completes the colorful country theme.

The simple pig motif can be adapted to decorate a whole range of household items with charming and colorful designs. Shown here are a few examples: a round wooden storage box, a cookie jar, terracotta pots, a tin bucket, and even decorative wall plaques and hangers.

·PAINTING·THE·SPOTTED·PIG·TRAY·

· Y O U · W I L L · N E E D ·

PAINTS
Satin-finish oil-based: medium-blue (base color), black
Tubes of artists' oils: black, red, white, cream, raw umber, green

BRUSHES
1in (2.5cm) flat, Nos. 1, 4, and 6 artist's, stencil

OTHER ITEMS
Tin tray, mineral spirits, cloth, pig outline (see page 121), sheet acetate, marker pen, cutting mat, craft knife, masking tape or repositionable spray glue, chalk, small white saucer, paint can or plate, antiquing medium or polyurethane varnish

---

1 Remove any labels with mineral spirits. Wash the tray in warm, soapy water and dry thoroughly. Using the 1in (2.5cm) flat brush, apply a coat of the base color to the tray's top surface and outer sides. To ensure an evenly painted surface, dip the brush head only ¼in (6mm) into the paint and apply with short, connecting strokes. When it is completely dry, add a second coat of base color, once again taking care to produce an even background. Let it dry.

2 Following the instructions on pages 14–15, copy and cut out the pig stencil on page 121. Holding it firmly in place with masking tape, paint over the stencil, using the stencil brush and black stain-finish paint. Make sure you pick up just a little paint on the brush, you can dab off any excess on a piece of paper. Allow the paint to dry a little before lifting off the stencil. Or, use the stencil as a template and simply draw around the inner edge with white chalk.

3 On a clean white saucer, make up the pig's body color by mixing a little red with white or cream, adding a tiny amount of raw umber. Once the stencil paint has dried, begin to paint the pig in more detail, following the step-by-step instructions on pages 24–25. Apply the body color first, then build up the details on top of it.

4 When you have completed the pig, and it has fully dried, begin the border design. To make a fairly even circle around the pig on which to paint the border of flowers and leaves, find an object slightly smaller than your tray—a paint can or plate will be fine. Draw a light circle around the edge with chalk.

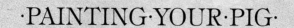

·PAINTING·YOUR·PIG·

1

Using the pig stencil, either draw or stencil the basic pig shape onto the prepared tray.

2

With the No. 6 artist's brush fill in the pig shape with the body color, add the tail as shown. Apply a second coat when it is dry, if required.

3

Add fine black lines, nostrils, mouth, and eye, using the No. 1 artist's brush.

4

Using the No. 4 artist's brush, add spots. Vary their size and keep them uneven in shape. Leave to dry thoroughly.

5

Following the contours of the pig as shown, lightly shade with the No. 4 artist's brush, using slightly thinned black paint. Shade and highlight following the instructions and tips on pages 12–13. Apply the paint sparingly, gradually building up the shading to avoid a heavy layer of paint.

6

With the No. 1 artist's brush, lightly highlight ears, nose, back, and tail in white. Leave to dry.

7

Draw a circle in chalk around the pig. Lightly mark where the flowers are to be placed. Paint the flowers with the No. 4 artist's brush using the mixed dark pink paint, then join them with a fine line of green. Paint leaves in green with the No. 4 brush (see pages 26–27).

5 Mark lightly where you want to place the flowers. Think of the tray as a clock face and paint the first flower at 12 o'clock, the second at 6 o'clock, then at 3 o'clock and 9 o'clock. Add other flowers between these points as you desire. Mix red with a small amount of white to create the petal color. Paint the flowers, using the No. 4 artist's brush and referring to page 16. Finally, fill in between the flowers with a leaf border, painted in green, using the No. 4 artist's brush.

6 Paint the back of the tray, using the base color. Leave to dry for approximately 24 hours. Once it is dry, you can either varnish the tray or antique it and then varnish the painted surface (see page 10). Apply varnish with a 1in (2.5cm) flat brush and let it dry in a dust-free environment. For an antiqued effect, use an antiquing medium (see page 10). Varnish the tray once it has been antiqued.

OTHER PIGS TO PAINT

There is always room for personalizing your projects by using a favorite breed or color of pig. Here are a couple of pigs in addition to the one on pages 20–21. The great advantage of the black pig (below) is that it doesn't need to be shaded, although, as you can see, a little highlighting enhances its shape. Its features need to be painted in a fine white. The eye must be done with particular care, or it will be completely lost. First highlight the eye area with white and then add the black eye. Even though the saddleback

pig (above) is also predominantly black, its pink belly will need shading.

The colors on the border can also be varied according to your choice. You might like to try a bright border around the pig. Or, rather than just one color, you might use two alternately, say, a russet brown and cream. Similarly, the leaves do not have to be done in green; they can be brown or gray. Try out different color combinations on paper. Once you have found one you are happy with, use it on the tray.

A bucket painted with a saddleback-pig motif. Use your pig stencil and adapt it, following the painting instructions above. Two shades of green have been used to create a vibrant background and border.

GOOSE WITH A TARTAN BOW TIE

This was one of the first items that I ever painted, and despite my lack of confidence and skill, I found that the bucket was transformed by the background color and its bold motif. The bucket's shape is also very effective for showing off roosters and other farm animals. The goose, with its smart tartan bow tie, has always been my favorite, and I particularly like the tartan pattern, which is surprisingly easy to paint. All you have to do is paint a few lines crossing each other at right angles.

Painting the inside of your bucket is optional, but it will be more versatile and functional if the inside is left unpainted because it can then be used for flowers, wood, water, or whatever else you care to put in it.

OVERLEAF   The goose is a popular and versatile motif, and it looks charming with or without a bow tie. Here you can see that I have varied the design by reversing it, changing the background color of the tie, and—just for a change—painting polka dots in a contrasting color in place of the tartan.

·PAINTING·THE·GOOSE·BUCKET·

·YOU·WILL·NEED·

PAINTS
Satin-finish oil-based: red (base color), gold
Tubes of artists' oils: white, yellow, green, black, red

BRUSHES
1½in (3.5cm) flat, Nos. 1, 4, and 6 artist's

OTHER ITEMS
Galvanized bucket (old or new), mineral spirits, soft cloth, sandpaper (optional), metal primer (optional), goose and tie outlines (see page 124), cutting mat, craft knife, masking tape or repositionable spray glue, chalk, high-gloss polyurethane varnish

1 Make sure your bucket has a spotlessly clean surface. First remove any labels with mineral spirits on a soft cloth and then dust the bucket. If the bucket is an old one, you may have to sand it down with a medium-grade sandpaper to remove any rust and apply a coat of primer. Following this, wash the bucket and then let it dry thoroughly.

2 Using the 1½in (3.5cm) flat brush, apply a coat of the red satin-finish paint. The galvanized surface takes the paint well, but it will need two coats, so let it dry overnight between coats. Take care when applying paint around the handles, as drips can occur. If you get any drips inside the bucket, wipe them off while the paint is wet, using a soft rag and mineral spirits.

3 Following the instructions on pages 14–15, copy and cut out the goose template on page 124. Position it firmly in place with the repositionable spray glue, remember to leave space for the goose's legs and feet at the bottom. Draw around the edge of the template with a piece of chalk and then paint the motif as detailed on pages 34–35.

4 The goose's bow tie is a separate template and needs to be prepared as in step 3. Position the template on the goose as described on the next page, draw around it with the chalk, and then paint.

PAINTING YOUR GOOSE

1

Fill the chalk outline, using the white paint and the No. 6 artist's brush. Two coats will probably be necessary, so allow time for both coats to dry.

2

For the beak, eyes, and feet, carefully chalk in the outlines. This gives you the opportunity to erase and try again if you find it difficult to get the proportions right. When you are happy with the outlines, fill them in with two coats of yellow paint, using the No. 4 artist's brush

3

Using the bow tie template, add a chalk outline of the bow tie at an appropriate part of the goose's neck, as shown on the previous page. Fill in the outline with green paint. Leave to dry thoroughly.

4

When the outline is dry, paint the details on the beak, eyes, wings, legs, and feet in black, using the No. 1 artist's brush.

5

To add the tartan lines to the bow tie, chalk in the grid as shown in diagram A (below) and then follow those lines with red artists' oil paint, using the No. 1 artist's brush. When the red paint is dry, paint along the edge of the red in yellow paint, again using the No. 1 artist's brush. Shade and highlight following the instructions and tips on pages 12–13.

Painting tartan lines on the bow tie

A

5. For a finishing touch, use an oil-based gold paint on the rim, base, and handle of the bucket. Paint it on with a No. 4 artist's brush. Use only small quantities of paint at a time to avoid any drips and runs. Leave to dry for approximately 24 hours.

6. Varnish the whole bucket with one coat of high-gloss polyurethane. Take particular care not to brush too much varnish over the gold paint, which can easily become tarnished in this way (see page 10 for guidance).

OTHER GEESE TO PAINT

There aren't too many ways of changing your goose in terms of color unless you are willing to embark upon a representation of some more exotic breed. To do this, search through books and magazines for a suit-able picture and use this as your outline and painting guide. If the picture you choose needs to be resized, use a photocopier to enlarge or re-duce the image.

To add some variety to the design featured here, or to per-sonalize your goose, you could use a different paint color for the bow tie. Or you could change the style of the tie by painting polka dots or a differ-ent tartan. Likewise you could give your bird a personalized garland of flowers and add a floral border to your project (see pages 16–17). This will create a different impression entirely.

Here the goose template has been used to decorate a tray – the egg template on page 124 creates the ideal border for the design.

BLACK ROOSTER

 These three mint-green tin containers are ideal for storing tea, coffee, and sugar. If you wish, you can paint the name of their contents in an appropriate place, on the lid for instance, or place an identifying sticker on the containers.

The handsome black roosters, with their red combs and faces, look at home in either a country kitchen or a more contemporary setting. The canisters I have used are inexpensive and, more important, are functional because the lid fits over a rim, rather than over the side of the tin, where it would scratch the painted surface. It is well worth bearing this in mind when you choose your storage containers.

The leaf-and-flower border is optional, but it goes well on the round tin containers. As an alternative to the black rooster on a light background, paint a white rooster on a dark background (see pages 40–41, and page 47), shading and highlighting in reverse of that described on page 45. It looks particularly dramatic.

OVERLEAF By combining the rooster with the egg, I have achieved all sorts of patterns here. Use eggs alone to make a border, as on the jug; paint them in pairs, as on the letter rack; or incorporate them into a leaf-and-flower border. Whatever you choose to do with the eggs, they will enliven the rooster motif—it is, after all, why he exists.

·PAINTING·THE·ROOSTER· ·STORAGE·CONTAINERS·

·YOU·WILL·NEED·

PAINTS
Satin-finish oil-based: pale green (base color)
Tubes of artists' oils: black, dark green, red, yellow, white, cream

BRUSHES
1½in (3.5cm) flat, Nos. 1, 4, and 6 artist's, stencil

OTHER ITEMS
Three tin storage containers, mineral spirits, clean cloth, rooster and egg outlines (see pages 120, 124), sheet acetate, marker pen, cutting mat, craft knife, masking tape or repositionable spray glue, pencil, chalk, gloss polyurethane varnish

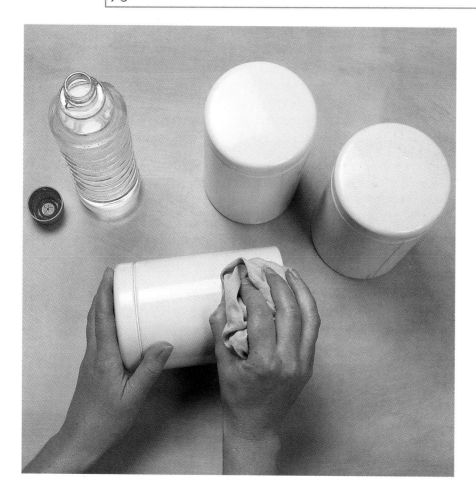

1. Make sure the containers are thoroughly clean before painting. If there are sticky labels on them, remove with mineral spirits on a clean cloth and then carefully dust the surface. Also, remove the lids from the pots before you begin to paint.

2 Using the 1½in (3.5cm) flat brush, carefully apply the first coat of the pale green base paint onto the pots and the lids and let it dry overnight. Apply the second coat of paint in the same way.

3 Following the instructions on pages 14–15, copy and cut out the rooster stencil on page 120. Position it firmly in place with repositionable spray glue and then paint over the stencil using the stencil brush and thinned black artists' oil paint. Let the paint dry and then continue to decorate the rooster as described on pages 44–45.

4 To put the egg on the lid, make a stencil from the egg outline on page 124 and position it as you did the rooster stencil. Fix it in place as in step 3, then stencil and paint as described on pages 44–45.

·PAINTING·YOUR·ROOSTER·

1

Fill in the stenciled area with another coat of black paint, using the No. 6 artist's brush. Add a little flourish of dark green paint on the tail, neck, and wing, also using the No. 6 brush. Leave to dry.

2

Using the red paint and the No. 4 artist's brush, fill in the rooster's comb and face.

3

Still using the No. 4 artist's brush, add the beak, eye and legs in yellow paint. Remember, you can pencil or chalk these in first in order to get the proportions right. Apply a second coat of yellow paint once the first has dried.

4

Using the No. 1 artist's brush and black paint, fill in the details on the eye, beak, comb, and legs.

5

Using the No. 1 artist's brush and slightly thinned white paint, add the white cheek and the detail of neck, wing, leg, and tail feathers.

6

The possibilities for adding shading to your rooster is limited on the black area, but can be done on the face and legs, as shown here.

7

Highlighting with white also makes an impact (follow the instructions and tips on pages 12–13). Pay particular attention to the tail, wing, and neck. Add the dot on the rooster's eye.

8

The egg in the center of the lid is stenciled with a cream artists' oil paint, thinned and then shaded around the edges to give it some depth. A white highlight will also give the impression of a sheen on the egg. As a final touch, add a border of flowers and leaves, as described on pages 16–17.

BLACK ROOSTER

5 Once the
roosters are
finished, add any
borders that you feel
are appropriate. For
the flowers, I have
mixed white with a
little red. Place them at
fairly regular intervals
around the top and
base of the container;
remember, the closer
together you paint the
flowers, the easier it
will be to join them
with an even border of
leaves.

6 Using the No. 1
artist's brush,
join each flower
to the next one with a
thin green line. Add
the leaves with the No.
6 artist's brush, as
described on page 16.
Once all the paint has
thoroughly dried
(approximately 24
hours), apply a single
coat of gloss
polyurethane varnish
to the storage
containers and their
lids.

OTHER ROOSTERS TO PAINT

There are three styles of rooster that I use regularly. The black one (as shown in the project), a white one, and a handsome colored one. For the white rooster, follow the instructions given for the black bird on pages 42–46, but substitute white paint for black.

To paint the colored rooster, use a dark green for the main body and highlight the tail with a little yellow. When that is dry, paint the wing in a rust color, then the neck and head in yellow, perhaps streaking the yellow with a little rust for depth. When the paint is dry, add the comb, beak, eye, and legs following Steps 3–4, as before. Continue to follow the instructions, and you will have a beautiful colored rooster.

Although these two roosters look very different, their outlines have been taken from the same stencil. To reverse a stencil, clean it thoroughly and then simply flip it over.

SHAGGY SHEEP

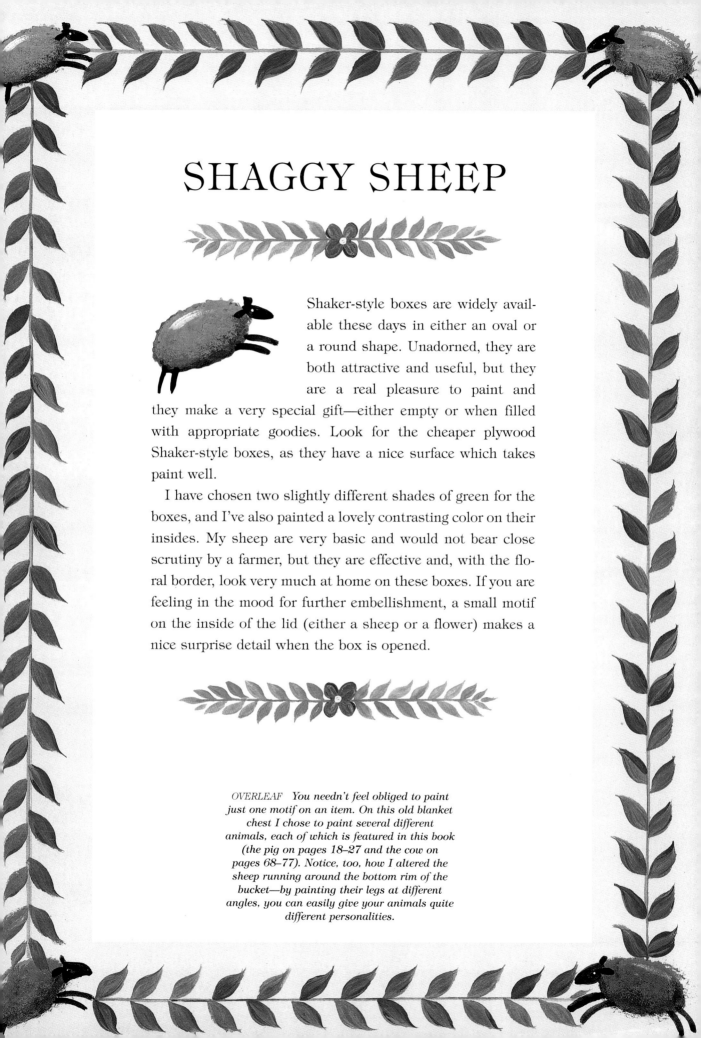

Shaker-style boxes are widely available these days in either an oval or a round shape. Unadorned, they are both attractive and useful, but they are a real pleasure to paint and they make a very special gift—either empty or when filled with appropriate goodies. Look for the cheaper plywood Shaker-style boxes, as they have a nice surface which takes paint well.

I have chosen two slightly different shades of green for the boxes, and I've also painted a lovely contrasting color on their insides. My sheep are very basic and would not bear close scrutiny by a farmer, but they are effective and, with the floral border, look very much at home on these boxes. If you are feeling in the mood for further embellishment, a small motif on the inside of the lid (either a sheep or a flower) makes a nice surprise detail when the box is opened.

OVERLEAF You needn't feel obliged to paint just one motif on an item. On this old blanket chest I chose to paint several different animals, each of which is featured in this book (the pig on pages 18–27 and the cow on pages 68–77). Notice, too, how I altered the sheep running around the bottom rim of the bucket—by painting their legs at different angles, you can easily give your animals quite different personalities.

·PAINTING·THE·SHEEP·SHAKER·BOX·

·YOU·WILL·NEED·

PAINTS
Acrylic or latex: black, brown, white, red, yellow, green

BRUSHES
1½in (3.5cm) flat, Nos. 1, 4, and 6 artist's, stencil

OTHER ITEMS
Shaker-style boxes made of wood (two, if possible), sheep outline (see pages 122–123), sheet acetate, marker pen, cutting mat, craft knife, masking tape or repositionable spray glue, chalk, pencil, sandpaper (fine-grade), satin acrylic varnish or antiquing medium

1 Paint the base color of your choice (here, a lovely grassy green) onto the boxes with the 1½in (3.5cm) brush. Use firm, even strokes, as only one coat of paint should be needed and it will dry within 30 minutes. Paint the bases and the lids separately because it will be easier to decorate them.

2 Paint the inside
of the box and
the lid, using
either the same color
as the outside or in a
contrasting color. Let
dry.

3 Following the
instructions on
pages 14–15,
copy and cut out a
sheep stencil from
pages 122–123.
Position it firmly in
place with the
repositionable spray
glue and then paint
over the stencil, using
the stencil brush and
black paint. Take care
with the spacing of the
figures around the
edges; the more evenly
spaced they are, the
better. Let the paint
dry and then continue
to decorate the sheep
as described on pages
54–55.

·PAINTING·YOUR·SHEEP·

1

After you have stenciled the sheep onto the lids and around the base, dip the stencil brush into brown, black, and white paints to paint the bodies. With a rhythmical stabbing motion, you can create a wonderful woolly effect. Keep building up the colors until you feel the sheep's wool looks right.

2

If you want to change the breed of sheep for your box, let it dry, then paint over the head and legs with white paint, using the No. 4 artist's brush.

3

Paint in the sheep's eyes and mouth, and the few lines that represent the joints and the feet. Use the No. 1 artist's brush to paint these details.

4

Shade and highlight the sheep following the instructions and tips on pages 12–13. Don't forget to add the sparkle in the sheep's eye.

5

For the border on the lid, mark guidelines as in step 4 on page 54. Then paint as in step 5 on page 26.

6

Join the flowers together with a thin green line, using the No. 1 artist's brush.

7

Add leaves, using the No. 4 artist's brush as described on page 16.

8

Add more flowers around the edge of the lid.

9

Join them together with a thin line.

10

Add leaves along the line you have just painted.

ANOTHER BORDER TO PAINT

Paint the sides of the lid in white, using the No. 6 brush.

In pencil, add zigzag lines.

Fill with black paint.

BORDER AROUND THE BASE

To make a border around the base of your box, first add flowers at regular intervals, then join with a thin green line, as before. Finally, add leaves.

4 When you have completed the sheep, and they have dried fully, begin the border design. To make an even circle around the sheep on which to paint the border of flowers and leaves, find a round object slightly smaller than your box lid—a paint can or plate will be fine. Draw a light chalk circle around the edge of this object.

5 When you are happy with the sheep and the borders, and the paint has completely dried, gently sand the edges of the boxes with fine grade sandpaper. This will antique them slightly.

6 Use the finish of your choice, such as a quick-drying satin acrylic varnish or an antiquing medium lightly rubbed onto the surface (or painted on and rubbed off; see page 10) to create a sheen and a protective coating for your boxes.

OTHER SHEEP TO PAINT

On this particular project I have varied the painting possibilities for the sheep by showing it with a black face and a white face and in a running or static position (see pages 50–51). Another way to vary the look of either the white- or the black-faced sheep is to add horns, thus turning it into a handsome ram. It is probably best to pencil or chalk in your horn shapes first and then mix a little yellow and brown to paint over your sketch.

Also illustrated here is a sheep with a lamb at its side. The lamb is quite simple to do and adds a very nice touch to the composition. Prepare a stencil using the motif given on page 122, and stencil the outline in place before painting the fully grown sheep. Otherwise, you will end up with wrong textures for the wool. When painting your lamb, note that it should not be quite as woolly as the fully grown adult sheep.

LEMONS AND PEARS

Painting unglazed terracotta is a very rewarding activity. Even without any embellishment, the porous surface takes water-based paints very well, and they dry so quickly that work isn't held up by waiting for the paint to dry.

On these dramatic black pots I have stenciled and painted both pears and lemons in a strongly contrasting yellow. The shading and highlighting of such fruit is very important; it gives them depth and that beautiful patina that so often appears, particularly on ripe pears.

Here, I have added a leaf border around the top of the pots and also pairs of leaves on each piece of fruit. Of course, lemons and pears seldom have leaves, so you may decide to paint the fruit without their leaves or, perhaps, paint a mixture—some with leaves, others without. Whichever pattern you choose, terracotta pots like these look stunning either on a sunroom windowsill or in a garden.

OVERLEAF As a slightly more sophisticated motif, the lemons and pears lend themselves to a variety of items and background colors. Here, they look equally good on green, Mediterranean blue, white, and dark blue. They also make useful border motifs and go particularly well with the Dove of Peace and Topiary Trees projects included in this book (see pages 78–87 and 98–107).

·PAINTING·THE·LEMON·AND·PEAR· ·TERRACOTTA·POTS·

·YOU·WILL·NEED·

PAINTS
Oil-based: gold (optional)
Acrylic or latex: black, yellow, white, green, brown (or raw umber and gold)

BRUSHES
1½in (3.5cm) flat, Nos. 1, 4 and 6 artist's, stencil

OTHER ITEMS
Two terracotta pots, mineral spirits, soft cloth, lemon and pear outlines (see page 123), sheet acetate, marker pen, cutting mat, craft knife, masking tape or repositionable spray glue, chalk, varnish or antiquing medium

1 Carefully dust the pots and remove any sticky labels (excess adhesive can be removed with some mineral spirits on a soft cloth). Then apply the base coat of black acrylic or latex paint using the 1½in (3.5cm) flat paintbrush. Only one coat will be needed. Remember to use short, even brush strokes as described on page 12.

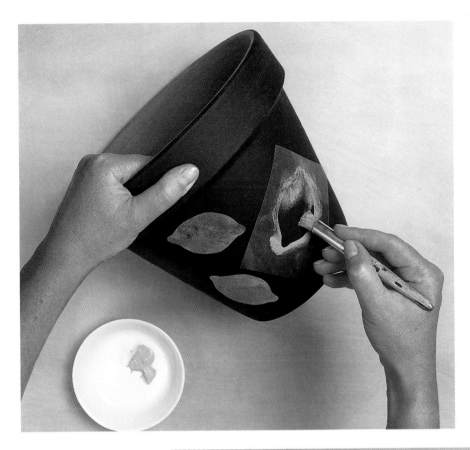

2. Following the instructions on pages 14–15, copy and cut out the lemon and pear stencils on page 123. When the base coat has dried (which is relatively quickly, depending on the weather), apply the stencils, positioning them firmly in place using repositionable spray glue. Then paint over the stencils, using the stencil brush and the yellow acrylic or latex paint.

3. Take care to apply the fruit at fairly even intervals. Place the stencils at random angles so the fruit looks more realistic. Let the paint dry and then continue to decorate the lemons and pears with shading and highlighting, as described on pages 64–65.

·PAINTING·YOUR·LEMONS·AND·PEARS·

1

When the stenciled
base coat is dry, the stencils
will be a pale yellow.

2

To enhance the coloring,
fill the stenciled shapes
with another coat of yellow
paint, but this time use the
No. 6 artist's brush. Follow
the natural contours of the
fruit with your brush
strokes.

3

Shade and highlight the
fruit following the
instructions and tips on
pages 12–13. Remember
that it is better to build up
the shading gradually than
to apply it too heavily in
the first place.

4

Add stalks and speckles
with dark brown or raw
umber, using the No. 4
artist's brush.

5

Using green paint with a
touch of yellow and a No. 4
artist's brush, paint the
leaves. The technique for
painting leaves is explained
more thoroughly on
page 16.

6

Prepare the leaf border as
described in step 4 (page
66). Then paint over the
chalk line, using green
paint and the No. 1 artist's
brush. Add leaves as above,
again using the No. 4
artist's brush.

4 To make the wavy leaf border on this pot, draw a line in chalk around the rim before painting and add leaves to each lemon with chalk as described. The advantage of roughing out a design in chalk is that if you make a mistake, you can easily erase it and draw again.

5 Once you are happy with your leaves and border outline, paint the leaf border as described on the previous page.

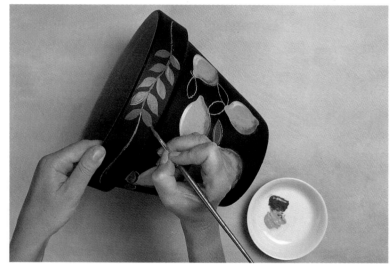

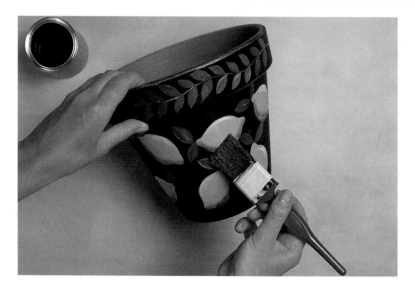

6 As an optional extra, adding gold as a border or onto the rim looks very dramatic in contrast to the black. Allow extra drying time before varnishing if you have added gold because the gold can easily become slightly tarnished-looking when varnish is applied too soon.

OTHER LEMONS AND PEARS TO PAINT

Although you can not vary the actual appearance of the lemon and pear motifs, you can alter the overall appearance by varying the background color and placement of the motifs. For the main project in this chapter they are placed at random on the terracotta pots, but with a little planning it is possible to paint the fruit in rows, even alternating them. To do this, you will have to divide the project into bands (use chalk or pencil), stencil your first fruit in place, and then use your stencil as a guide to see how many you can fit onto the project. As you can see, I have joined together the lemons and pears with leaves. For details on painting borders, see pages 16–17.

COW AND
WHEAT SHEAF

 The best thing about bread boxes is that you don't have to use them to store bread. I have one for pasta, one for flour, and one for dog biscuits. Furthermore, there are many old enamel bread boxes to be found, and this is the perfect project for one that is in need of a face-lift.

Although I have a weakness for the more traditional black-and-white or brown-and-white cows, I thought that this chocolate brown cow on the antiqued creamy background made a slightly more subtle combination. Once you have your cow stencil, though, you can paint whichever breed of cow most appeals to you.

The wheat sheaves on the lid and on the box itself are simple to paint and add some welcome lightness to this design. Because the cow's body is so long, it is all too easy for this design to become a little dense, so if you decide to paint a similarly colored animal, be sure to paint it onto a pale colored background.

OVERLEAF Varying the look of your cows is very straightforward. Outline areas of color on the background with a piece of chalk or a pencil. Once you are happy with the shapes, simply fill them in, using a No. 4 artist's paintbrush. For particularly fine spots, use a No. 1 brush.

·PAINTING·THE·COW·BREAD·BOX·

·YOU·WILL·NEED·

PAINTS
Satin-finish oil-based: magnolia, gold (optional), black
Tubes of artists' oils: black, brown, white, red, yellow, green

BRUSHES
1½in (3.5cm) flat, Nos. 1, 4, and 6 artist's, stencil

OTHER ITEMS
Enamel bread box, mineral spirits, soft cloth, sandpaper (medium-grade optional), metal primer (optional), cow outline (see page 119), sheet acetate, marker pen, cutting mat, craft knife, repositionable spray glue, antiquing medium, gloss polyurethane varnish

1 *Make sure your bread box is spotlessly clean. Remove any labels with mineral spirits on a soft cloth and then carefully dust it. If the bread box is an old one, you may have to sand it down with medium-grade sandpaper to remove any rust and apply a coat of primer. Following this preparation, wash the bread box and then let it dry thoroughly.*

2 Apply the first coat of the magnolia satin-finish paint, using the 1½in (3.5cm) flat brush. Paint it on carefully and sparingly to avoid drips, especially around the handles. Let the paint dry thoroughly and then apply a second coat of paint.

3 Following the instructions on pages 14–15, copy and cut out the cow stencil on page 119. Position it firmly in place with the repositionable spray glue and then paint over the stencil, using the stencil brush and black satin-finish paint. Make sure you pick up just a little paint on the brush. Continue to paint the rest of the cow as described on pages 14–15.

·PAINTING·YOUR·COW·

1

Mix brown paint with a little white to make a soft brown color. Carefully paint onto the stenciled area, using the No. 6 artist's brush for the body; but change to the smaller No. 4 brush for the legs, tail, and head. Leave to dry.

2

Mix some antique pink (white with very small amounts of red and brown) and paint the cow's muzzle and udder, using the No. 4 artist's brush.

3

Using the No. 1 artist's brush and black paint, add detail lines as shown. Use the dark brown paint and the No. 4 artist's brush for the cow's hooves.

4

If you wish to add horns to the cow, use a mixture of brown and yellow paints. Chalk in the horns first as a guideline for your paintbrush. You may find that they require two coats. Allow the paint to dry thoroughly.

5

Your cow should now be ready for shading. Pay particular attention around the udder, chin, and legs.

6

Carefully highlight appropriate parts of your cow with a little thinned white paint.

7

To create the grassy effect under the cow's hooves, use the stencil brush to stipple green paint with some yellow highlights. To create this effect, put a very small amount of both colors on the brush and use short stabbing movements.

TO PAINT THE WHEAT MOTIF

Copying the image illustrated, lightly pencil in the wheat motif in the size you require for your project. Use a No. 1 brush for the stalks and a No. 4 brush for the ears and leaves. Use a tiny amount of brown with the yellow, as this adds depth to the color and image.

4 After you have finished painting the cow, add the wheat motif as desired. In this case, I have positioned it on the lid. Paint the motif as described on the previous page.

5 Decorate the bread box handles with either the gold paint or a contrasting color. The rim of the lid and the handle on the lid should also be painted to match.

6 I have also added an extra inner border of red around the rim of the lid. Painted on with a No. 4 artist's brush, the inner border is a useful way of disguising any wobbly or ragged edges in the trim color. Once all the paint has dried thoroughly, antique the surface quite heavily with antiquing medium before applying a gloss polyurethane varnish. (If you have used gold paint, see page 10 for information about varnishing over gold.)

OTHER COWS TO PAINT

One of the easiest ways to vary your cow outline is to turn it into a sleeping cow. The cow at the right on the box lid shows just such a resting cow. The outline should be quite easy to copy and position on your bread box, or on any other object you decorate.

Once you have your basic cow outline, whether it is the one featured on the previous pages or the one at the right, it is quite simple to draw patches onto a white background and create your own black-and-white, brown-and-white, beige-and-white or even terracotta-and-white cow.

To do this effectively, it is best to paint one or two coats of white onto your stenciled shape and then pencil in the patches in the appropriate places. By penciling them in, you can easily fix the patches if you find that they are too big, too small, or in the wrong place. Paint the patches and finish off by filling in the muzzle and udder with pink.

This hatbox has been decorated with cows charging around a field and one rather sleepy beast. Such variations are fun to create, and they give originality to your designs.

DOVE OF PEACE

 Of the 10 projects shown in this book, I think that this is my favorite. The dove motif is one of the simplest to do and works well with flowers and leaves, as the canister standing atop the chest of drawers shows. On the unit itself, I have used simple line and dot borders on the drawers and surrounding base. However, if you prefer a more floral effect, flowers painted at the corner of each drawer and joined together with a leaf border look very pretty around the dove. For details on painting this border and for some other ideas, see pages 16–17.

Because the chest of drawers that I used came in a basic white wood, I was able to paint directly onto it with water-based paint. I chose a warm rusty red which contrasts well with the white birds and the green trim. For a variation in color, I painted the insides of the drawers in the same green as the trim.

OVERLEAF The beauty of stencil designs is that they can be enlarged or reduced very easily (see page 15) to suit your project. The blue card with green border on the left uses the dove in two different sizes, and the wooden box at the top uses three sizes. The dove also works very well with other designs in this book, particularly the pears that appear on pages 58–67.

·PAINTING·THE·DOVE·CHEST·OF·DRAWERS·

> ### ·YOU·WILL·NEED·
>
> *PAINTS*
> Acrylic or latex: rust red, white, yellow, black, green
>
> *BRUSHES*
> 1½in (3.5cm) flat, Nos. 1, 4, and 6 artist's, stencil
>
> *OTHER ITEMS*
> Small wooden chest of drawers (unfinished wood, with no paint or varnish), sandpaper (medium-grade), clean cloths, mineral spirits, dove outline (see page 126), sheet acetate, marker pen, cutting mat, craft knife, masking tape or repositionable spray glue, ruler, pencil, antiquing medium

1 Remove all of the drawers and prepare them and the surrounding areas by sanding down any rough edges with medium-grade sandpaper and then dust with a damp cloth. If there is any sticky residue left by labels, remove it with mineral spirits on a cloth.

2 Using the 1½in (3.5cm) brush, paint the fronts, sides, and upper edges of each drawer and the shell with the acrylic or latex base coat. I used different colors for the drawers and the shell, but you may decide to use the same one for both. By using short, even strokes, you should need only one coat of base color.

3 Following the instructions on pages 14–15, copy and cut out one of the dove stencils on page 126. Position it firmly in place using the repositionable spray glue and then paint over the stencil, using the stencil brush and white acrylic or latex paint.

4 To reverse the dove design, cut out and use the other dove stencil from page 126. Alternatively, wipe the side of the stencil that you have been using to remove any paint residue and then flip over the stencil and use as before. Continue to paint the dove as described on pages 84–85.

·PAINTING·YOUR·DOVE·

1

Stencil on the dove outline
using the stencil brush and
white paint.

2

Add the beak and eyes, using
the No. 4 artist's brush and
the yellow paint.

3

Using the No. 1 artist's brush
and the black paint, carefully
paint the details on the beak,
eye, wings, and tail. If you
prefer, you can pencil these
in first.

4

Shade the dove following
the instructions and tips on
pages 12–13. Try to do this
as delicately as possible
because the black contrasts so
strongly with the white.

5

With a ruler and a pencil, draw lines around the edge of each drawer. Measure approximately ¼in (6mm) from the edge of the drawers.

6

When you have drawn all the lines, paint over them with green paint, using the No. 4 artist's brush.

7

Add colored dots within the border made by the drawer's edge and the lines you have just painted. Dots can be surprisingly difficult to paint, so practice first on a piece of scrap paper.

8

As an optional extra, add leaves to the dove designs that appear on the top and sides of the chest of drawers. Pencil in the stem first, paint over the top in green, and then paint the leaves (see page 16).

5 To create some decorative details, paint a fine line ½in (12mm) in from the edge all around the drawer fronts. Finish with small dots painted in a contrasting color.

6 To finish and seal the chest of drawers, brush on antiquing medium and then wipe off most of the excess with a soft cloth (see page 10). Don't forget to do this on the sides of the drawers, too.

OTHER DOVES TO PAINT

There aren't too many ways that you can change the look of your flying dove. However, the style of border you add to the project can make a great difference to the overall appearance. In the project illustrated on the previous pages, I have tried not to let the design become fussy or floral, but by adding lots of flowers and leaves, you can make a very pretty project. You could also add some fruit, such as lemons, and pears (see pages 62–68 for painting instructions), to the border. These can look very attractive with your lovely flying dove.

Doves are just as happy standing still as soaring through the air. Use the dove to the left as an outline for a template and paint it on a jar just like the one shown below.

You can use the soaring dove from the project to decorate your jar, or re-create the design on page 4 by painting a garland around the dove. This would be ideal decoration for a round tray or a lid.

AURICULA PRIMROSE

Over the past few years, the auricula primrose has become increasingly popular. It can be found decorating many a household item, including wallpapers and fabrics. Auriculas are unusual plants and quite difficult to grow successfully in their pure form. Perhaps this elusive charm is what makes the painted items so sought after. The flowers come in a variety of wonderful deep colors, and my interpretation rather simplifies the richness and beauty of the plant. In combination with the blue-and-white pot, however, the effect is lovely; you can choose your background to complement your favorite color flower.

I like these Victorian-looking enamel jugs and feel that they are suitably elegant in shape to carry this particular design. When completed, your jug can be used for flowers. If you use it as a beverage container, though, treat it with care, as enamel jugs are vulnerable to chipping when used everyday.

OVERLEAF For variety, the flower heads can be different colors, of course, and you can have great fun developing all sorts of patterns to decorate the pots, too. Notice the small pots above the cupboard to the left of the picture: they feature just the auricula heads and some leaves, making a charmingly simple design.

·PAINTING·THE·AURICULA·PRIMROSE·JUG·

· Y O U · W I L L · N E E D ·

PAINTS
Satin-finish oil-based: navy blue (base color), gold
Tubes of artists' oils: white, black or raw umber, blue, green, yellow

BRUSHES
1½in (3.5cm) flat, Nos. 1, 4, and 6 artist's, stencil

OTHER ITEMS
Enamel jug, auricula pot outline (see page 123), sheet acetate,
marker pen, cutting mat, craft knife, masking tape or repositionable
spray glue, pencil, chalk, mineral spirits, gloss polyurethane varnish

---

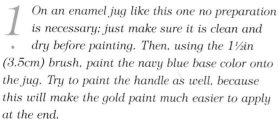

1 *On an enamel jug like this one no preparation is necessary; just make sure it is clean and dry before painting. Then, using the 1½in (3.5cm) brush, paint the navy blue base color onto the jug. Try to paint the handle as well, because this will make the gold paint much easier to apply at the end.*

2 *To finish the jug neatly, turn it upside down and paint the base, using the same navy blue paint. The jug can be left upside down to dry. For a neater finish, the jug will need two coats of paint. Before applying the second coat, allow the first to dry overnight.*

3 Following the
instructions on
pages 14–15,
copy and cut out the
auricula pot stencil
on page 123. Position
it firmly in place
toward the bottom of
the jug with the
repositionable spray
glue and then paint
over the stencil, using
the stencil brush and
thinned white artists'
oil paint.

4 When the paint
has dried, remove
the stencil and
apply another coat of
the white paint over
the pot. Then decorate
the jug as described on
pages 94–95.

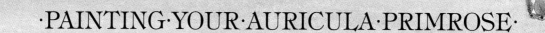

·PAINTING·YOUR·AURICULA·PRIMROSE·

1

Paint a second coat of white paint over the stenciled pot outline.

2

When the white paint is dry, sketch an oval shape and fill with either the black or the raw umber paint to represent soil. Use the No. 4 artist's brush.

3

Once the paint is dry, decorate the pot with the blue paint. First pencil the design lightly onto the pot and then paint over the lines, using the No. 4 artist's brush and slightly thinned blue paint (this makes a slightly less opaque finish). Add blue dots around the rim and the base.

4

When you have finished painting the blue pattern onto the white pot, and it has dried, shade along the sides and top and base. Shade following the instructions and tips given on page 12.

5

Find the center of the pot; from there, chalk in a slightly curving stalk approximately 2½in (6cm) high. Once you are satisfied with it, paint it, using the green paint, slightly lightened with white, and the No. 4 artist's brush.

6

For the auricula primrose, study my picture and then arrange a group of flower heads around the top of the stalk. Sketch them first with chalk.

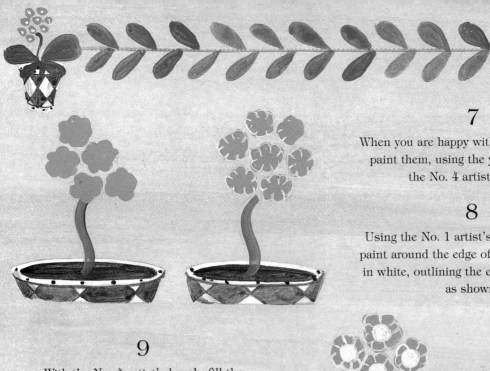

7

When you are happy with the proportions, paint them, using the yellow paint and the No. 4 artist's brush.

8

Using the No. 1 artist's brush, carefully paint around the edge of each flower head in white, outlining the edge of each petal as shown.

9

With the No. 4 artist's brush, fill the center of each flower with white.

10

When the white paint is dry, fill with yellow as shown. It should look a little like a poached egg.

11

Next, pencil or chalk in the leaves so that the larger ones reach out beyond the pot and the smaller ones creep over the front edge. Paint them, using the green paint and either the No. 4 or the No. 6 brush.

12

Outline the leaves in white, using the No. 1 artist's brush. Finally, place a tiny white dot in the center of each flower.

13

To add some depth to the leaves, shade a little at the base of the leaves and stalk, as described on page 12.

14

Highlight the leaves quite heavily (as described on page 13) to represent the characteristic whiteness that appears on auricula leaves.

5. *For some of the other projects in this book, I have suggested an optional gold trim for the handles and rims. But for this auricula primrose, I recommend the addition of some gold, as it enhances the formality, and hence the attractiveness, of the composition. After applying the gold, leave to dry for approximately 24 hours.*

6. *Add a coat of gloss poly-urethane varnish to bring out the beautiful colors of your handsome jug. See page 10 for advice on varnishing over gold oil-based paint, which can all too easily become tarnished-looking.*

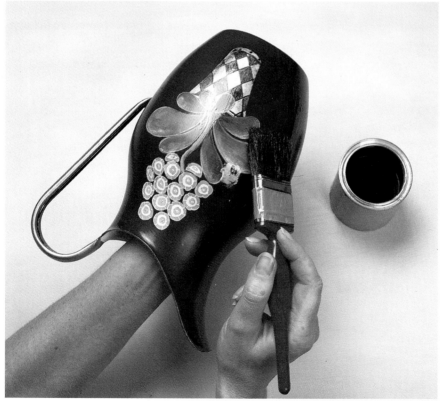

OTHER AURICULA PRIMROSES TO PAINT

The most obvious way of changing or varying your auricula design is to use a different color for the flower. Study botanical pictures and photographs and then interpret them in a simplified form for your painting. A deep red color looks beautiful; instead of edging the petals with a fine white line, use pink so that the edging doesn't contrast too sharply with the deep color of the petal.

Another variation is to put your plant in a plain terracotta pot instead of the blue-and-white pot featured on the previous pages. You can always add some interest to your terracotta by aging it. Add some hairline "cracks" with a No. 1 brush and some raw umber paint and then, before shading and highlighting, put a little thinned green paint on your fingertip and dab onto the terracotta to create a moss or lichen effect.

Paint your auricula flower heads in any shade and add as many or as few leaves as you like. Change the length of the stem, too: there is no need to be afraid to adapt these designs.

TOPIARY TREES

 There is a classic timelessness to this simple topiary motif that makes it fit in with many themes and settings. When I was planning this particular design, I felt that the watering can would make an extremely good background because of its use in the garden. I also found that the taller shape accommodates the trees perfectly. As with the Goose With A Tartan Bow Tie (see pages 28–37), a template of the tree may be easier to use than a stencil. The ridges commonly found in galvanized-metal ware can make stenciling quite tricky, and it is easier to hold a template steady. Once you have drawn the motif's outline, all you then have to do is fill it in.

Some highlighting and shading on the trees and pots is particularly essential to prevent them from looking too flat. The small amount of white highlighting gives the pots and their trees an authentic sheen, as if they were standing in the garden on a sunny day.

OVERLEAF With its garden theme, the topiary design lends itself to items for the garden or greenhouse such as terracotta pots, watering cans, and containers for all those small but essential pieces of gardening equipment. On some of these items I have chosen to decorate the topiary tree containers with blue-and-white patterns for a bit of variety.

·PAINTING·THE·TOPIARY·WATERING·CAN·

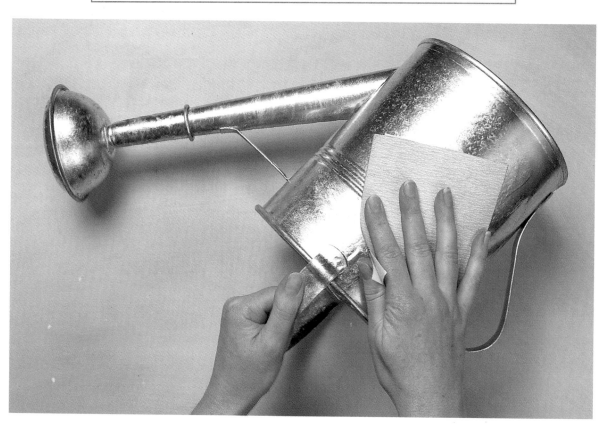

1 *Make sure your watering can has a meticulously clean surface. First remove any labels with mineral spirits on a soft cloth and then dust. If the watering can is an old one, you may have to sand it down with medium-grade sandpaper to remove any rust and apply a coat of primer. Finally, wash the watering can and then let it dry thoroughly.*

2 *Paint on the first coat of the wheat base color, using the 1½in (3.5cm) brush. There will be some awkward little spots on the watering can, so take care, particularly under the handles and around the spout and the rose. Watch out for drips, although this problem should not occur if you use only a small amount of paint on the brush. Let the watering can dry overnight before you apply the second coat of base color.*

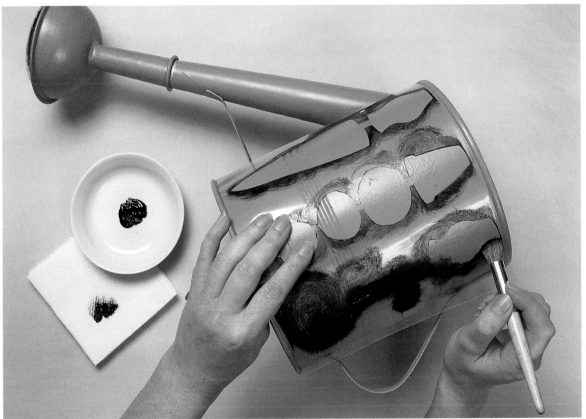

3 *Following the instructions on pages 14–15, copy and cut out the topiary motif on page 118. Position it firmly in place with the repositionable spray glue and then paint over the stencil, using the stencil brush and black satin-finish paint. Make sure you have only a little paint on the brush. Finally, paint the motifs as described in detail on pages 104–105.*

·PAINTING·YOUR·TOPIARY·

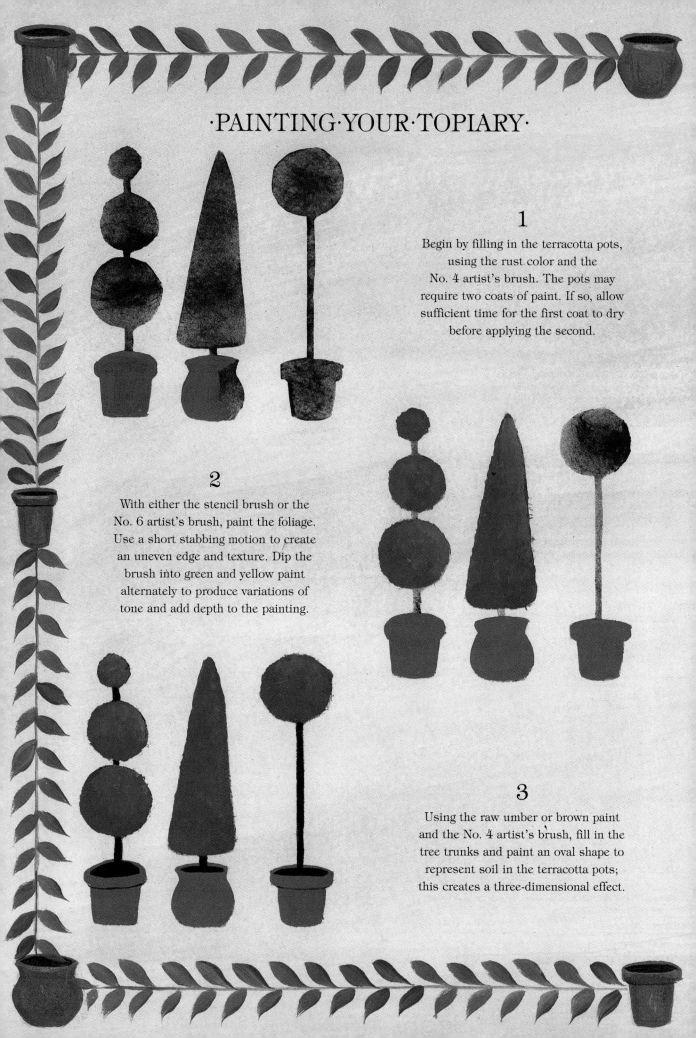

1

Begin by filling in the terracotta pots, using the rust color and the No. 4 artist's brush. The pots may require two coats of paint. If so, allow sufficient time for the first coat to dry before applying the second.

2

With either the stencil brush or the No. 6 artist's brush, paint the foliage. Use a short stabbing motion to create an uneven edge and texture. Dip the brush into green and yellow paint alternately to produce variations of tone and add depth to the painting.

3

Using the raw umber or brown paint and the No. 4 artist's brush, fill in the tree trunks and paint an oval shape to represent soil in the terracotta pots; this creates a three-dimensional effect.

4

Shade and highlight the pots and topiary trees as illustrated. This will greatly enhance their depth. For instructions and tips on shading and highlighting, see pages 12–13.

5

To add even more interest to your trees, you can add lemons and pears, as shown in the project on pages 58–67.

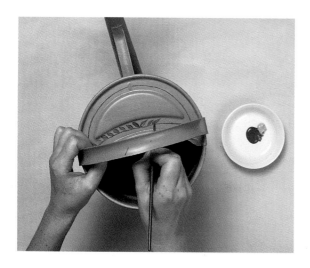

4 To decorate the top of the watering can, paint a thin green line and add leaves as described on page 16.

5 Carefully paint the edges of the watering can with the gold paint. If gold is not available, use green or rust; either one will complement the design. Two coats are usually needed.

6 When the paint is completely dry, antique and then varnish the watering can. If you have used gold paint, see page 10 for advice on varnishing over gold which can easily become tarnished-looking.

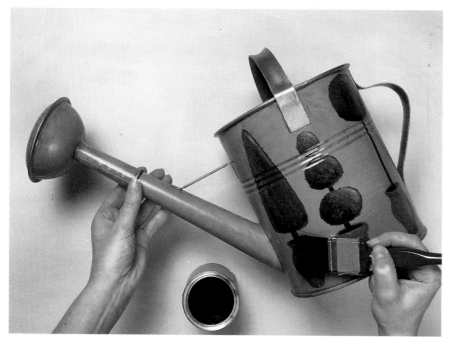

OTHER TOPIARY TO PAINT

I love the simplicity of the topiary motif, but there are some straightforward ways to make it a little more elaborate. First, instead of the plain terracotta pots, you could create blue-and-white pots by following the instructions given for the pot in the Auricula Primrose project (see pages 88–97). In addition, put lemons or pears on your trees to add some color and create a completely different look. Sketch your fruits first and then paint in the color required. When the paint is dry, shade and highlight the fruit.

CHINA TEAPOT

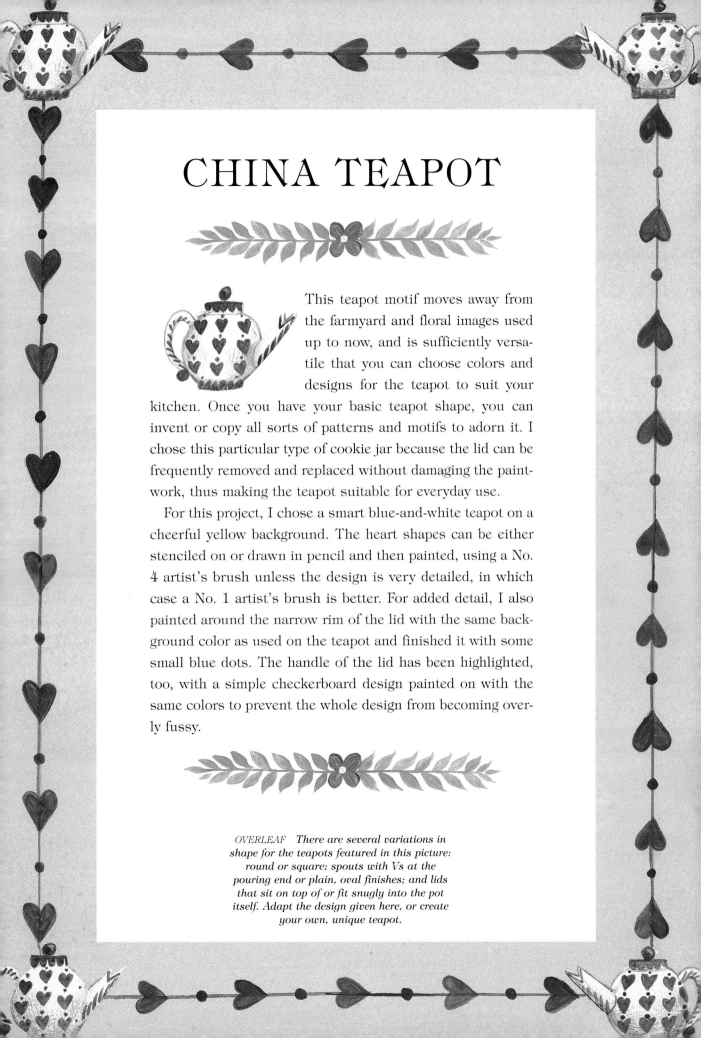

This teapot motif moves away from the farmyard and floral images used up to now, and is sufficiently versatile that you can choose colors and designs for the teapot to suit your kitchen. Once you have your basic teapot shape, you can invent or copy all sorts of patterns and motifs to adorn it. I chose this particular type of cookie jar because the lid can be frequently removed and replaced without damaging the paintwork, thus making the teapot suitable for everyday use.

For this project, I chose a smart blue-and-white teapot on a cheerful yellow background. The heart shapes can be either stenciled on or drawn in pencil and then painted, using a No. 4 artist's brush unless the design is very detailed, in which case a No. 1 artist's brush is better. For added detail, I also painted around the narrow rim of the lid with the same background color as used on the teapot and finished it with some small blue dots. The handle of the lid has been highlighted, too, with a simple checkerboard design painted on with the same colors to prevent the whole design from becoming overly fussy.

OVERLEAF   There are several variations in shape for the teapots featured in this picture: round or square; spouts with Vs at the pouring end or plain, oval finishes; and lids that sit on top of or fit snugly into the pot itself. Adapt the design given here, or create your own, unique teapot.

·PAINTING·THE·TEAPOT·COOKIE·JAR·

·YOU·WILL·NEED·

PAINTS
Satin-finish oil-based: yellow (base color)
Tubes of artists' oils: white, black, blue

BRUSHES
1½in (3.5cm) flat, Nos. 1, 4, and 6 artist's, stencil

OTHER ITEMS
Metal cookie jar (old or new, with a lid that fits inside rather than outside), mineral spirits, clean cloth, teapot outline (see page 125), sheet acetate, marker pen, cutting mat, craft knife, masking tape or repositionable spray glue, pencil, antiquing medium, polyurethane varnish (satin or gloss)

 Before beginning to paint the cookie jar, make sure it is meticulously clean. If there is any residue from sticky labels, gently remove it with some mineral spirits on a clean piece of cloth.

Remove the lid from the cookie jar and paint on the first coat of the base color on the outside only—do not paint the inside of the lid. The jar will need two coats of paint, so let it dry overnight before applying the second coat.

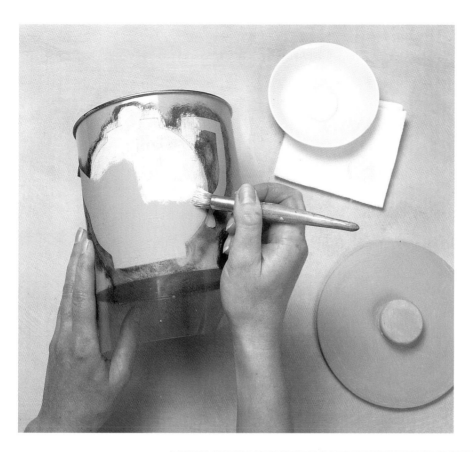

3 *Following the instructions on pages 14–15, copy and cut out the teapot stencil on page 125. Position it firmly in place with the repositionable spray glue. Then paint over the stencil, using the stencil brush and thinned white artists' oil paint. Continue to paint the rest of the teapot as described on pages 114–115.*

4 *To decorate the cookie jar lid, paint the knob and trim in a contrasting color. You can stencil hearts around the top of the lid, as shown on page 112. Fill in the stenciled shapes using the No. 4 artist's brush.*

·PAINTING·YOUR·TEAPOT·

1

Fill in your teapot stencil, using the No. 6 artist's brush and white artists' oil paint. One coat should be enough.

2

Paint the lines around the lid, spout, and handle using the No. 1 artist's brush and black paint. This will help to give the teapot its rotund shape.

3

Using the pencil, lightly sketch the design onto the teapot. The hearts and other decor do not have to be placed at precise distances from each other.

4

When you are happy with the proportions of the decorations, paint them, using the blue paint and the No. 4 artist's brush. Leave to dry.

5

Carefully shade and highlight the teapot following the instructions and tips on pages 12–13. Pay particular attention to the areas around the spout and the handles. Add a little highlight to the teapot's knob.

DECORATING THE LID

Pencil in the design, paint in white, and then add decorative details in blue.

5 Painting a contrasting line around the edges of the hearts will help them to complement the teapot's colors. Place dots around the rim of the lid. Leave the project to dry for approximately 24 hours.

6 Finish this project with antiquing medium and satin or gloss polyurethane varnish (see page 10 for more information).

OTHER TEAPOTS TO PAINT

Once you have your basic teapot shape, you can use it as a canvas and paint onto it any number of designs or patterns, either simple or complex. One possibility is to combine the teapot design with another of the projects featured in this book. For example, you could paint your basic teapot in a color other than white and paint onto it a rooster or auricula primrose (you can always reduce your trace-off motif to fit your teapot shape). The illustration shows one teapot that has been decorated in this way, combining the rooster with different borders.

The teapot above features the rooster from pages 38–47 and also makes great fun of combining borders of many different styles.

The delicate dove motif from pages 78–87 forms the central image on the teapot below which has been given an antique finish.

TRACE-OFF MOTIFS

The trace-off motifs given on these pages (118–126) are for each of the projects in this book. For information on using the motifs to make stencils and templates, and sizing them to fit your project, see pages 14–15. Some of the animals, such as the roosters on page 120 and the sheep on pages 122–123, appear in a variety of positions from which you can select your favorite.

TOPIARY TREES

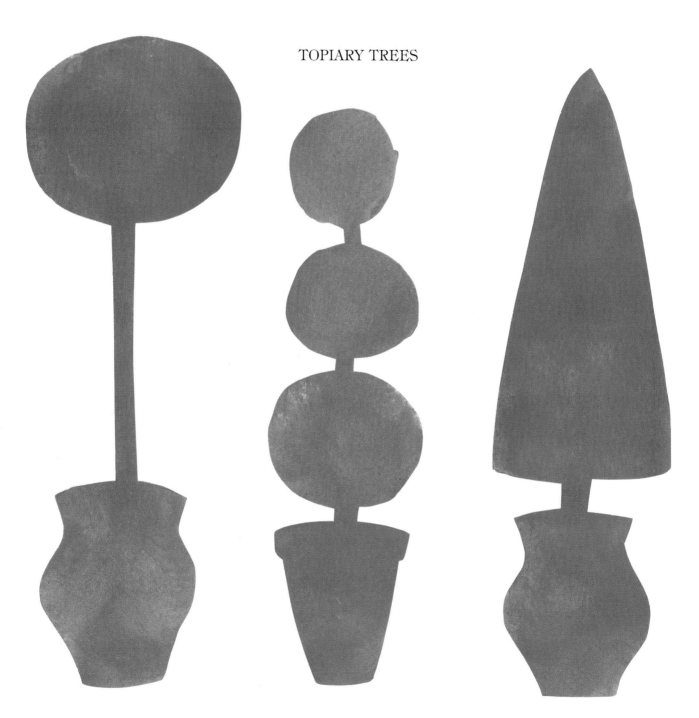

COW

ROOSTERS

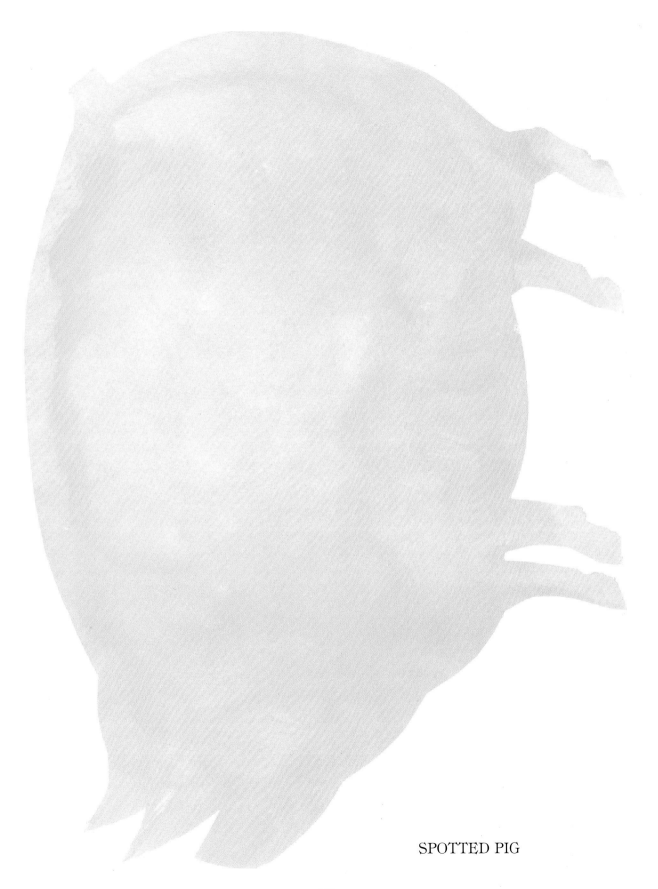

SPOTTED PIG

SHAGGY SHEEP

SHAGGY SHEEP

LEMONS AND PEARS

AURICULA PRIMROSE POT

GOOSE WITH A TARTAN BOW TIE

CHINA TEAPOT

DOVE OF PEACE

INDEX